THE BUG CLUB BOOK

The luna moth

THE BUG CLUB BOOK

A HANDBOOK FOR *YOUNG BUG* COLLECTORS

N 9

by

Gladys Conklin

Illustrated by

Girard Goodenow

HOLIDAY HOUSE—NEW YORK

The chapter "A NOTE TO PARENTS AND TEACHERS"
is reprinted, in somewhat different form,
from *Junior Libraries,* November 1959,
published by R. R. Bowker Company.

Contents

for IRVING,
who has learned to live with the
changing assortment of caterpillar jars
on the kitchen table

Bugs All Around

Bugs are the most astonishing animals on this earth. Most people do not think of them as animals, but all living things are divided into two big groups, the plant kingdom and the animal kingdom.

There are more bugs, or insects, in the world than all other animals put together. About 900,000 different kinds of insects are known, and thousands more are being described by scientists each year.

Bugs are found everywhere. They are crawling, hopping, and flying in every kind of place imaginable. They are found in sunny meadows, on icy mountain tops, and in dark, damp caves. They have a strange and dramatic life that has stirred the imagination of man for thousands of years.

Right in your own back yard there could be as many

as 500 to 1,000 different kinds of insects. A scientist, Frank E. Lutz, of the American Museum of Natural History, tried an experiment in his own yard, about 75 feet wide and 200 feet long. He found 1,402 different kinds of insects that either lived in his yard or flew into it.

Imagine finding 1,402 different kinds of bugs in one yard! It doesn't seem possible, does it? How many kinds did you see today? Grasshoppers? Katydids? Bees? Butterflies? Skippers? Ants? Crickets? Why don't you keep a list and challenge one of your friends to keep one, too? See who can have the longest list in one day, or in a week, or at the end of summer vacation.

While you are keeping this list, you will see the most unusual things. It will be your lucky day when you see a shiny black wasp dragging a caterpillar across the yard. She has already dug a little hole in the ground and wants to take the caterpillar down into the small cave. The caterpillar is not dead, only paralyzed, for the wasp has partly poisoned it. The wasp tugs at the limp body and pushes it around until it is in the right position, then pulls it quickly underground and out of sight. Don't go away. The wasp will lay an egg on the caterpillar and then come out. Now you will witness an amazing feat. If someone told you that a wasp could pound with a stone, would you believe it? Watch and see what happens right before your eyes. The wasp quickly tumbles dirt down into the hole until it is full. Then she buzzes around until she finds a pebble just the right size and shape. With the pebble grasped in her mouth parts, she pounds the earth down

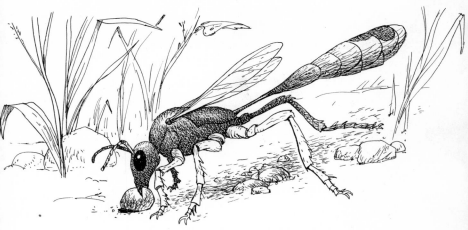

A sphecid wasp using a "tool"

into the hole until it is smooth and level with the ground around it. Then off she flies to dig another hole, find another caterpillar, and lay another egg.

Underground, the egg will hatch in a few days into a grub which will feed on the caterpillar. In a week or so this grub will spin a cocoon around its body and, in time, come out as a shiny black wasp. If it is a female, she will start the hole-caterpillar-egg cycle all over again.

If there is a sandy area near your house, take a jar and an old spoon and hunt for the homely doodlebug. Look for tiny cone-shaped pits in the sand. The doodlebug hides at the bottom of a pit with only a sharp pair of pincers barely visible. Scoop quickly under the pit with your spoon and sprinkle the dirt out on the ground. Look carefully because the doodlebug resembles a gray lump of dirt, until he moves. Drop to your knees and watch him. When he starts to work, he moves rapidly, and always backwards. As he digs his pit he throws the dirt out with the back of his head. He travels in circles that grow shorter and shorter as he spirals to the bottom. Without seeing what he is doing, he shapes a pit as perfectly as if it had been done with a machine. When the size suits him, he settles down at the bottom and waits for the first careless ant to come along. When an ant slips over the edge, the soft sand slides and carries him to the bottom and into a pair of waiting jaws.

Scoop up one of the doodlebugs and take him home in a jar of sand. Doodlebugs, which are larvas, live in the ground for two years, so dig up several and choose the largest one. When you leave him undisturbed, he will rebuild his pit in your jar. For food, drop ants or gently swatted flies into the pit. The doodlebug quickly sucks out all the juice from the body, then flips the remains completely out of the hole.

Some morning when you look, there will be no pit in the sand. Wait four or five days, then carefully sift the sand with an old tea strainer. The cocoon of the doodlebug will be a small, round sandy ball. How does he manage to spin a cocoon around himself while buried in the sand? It sounds almost like dressing in deep water without getting wet. Leave the cocoon in the sand and fasten a piece of net or old nylon stocking over the jar if you want to see the adult when it comes out. Be sure to place a few twigs or sticks in the jar for the ant lion to climb upon to dry its wings. The ant lion, adult of the doodlebug, looks like a sturdy little damselfly with knobby antennae.

Can you always recognize an insect when you see one? A typical insect has six jointed legs and a body composed of three parts: head, thorax, and abdomen. But all insects are not typical. Sometimes the first two legs don't show plainly, and the body may look as if it has two parts instead of three. This you will learn by experience.

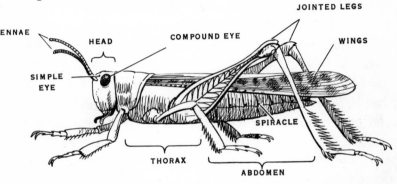

The outer parts of a typical insect, shown on a grasshopper. The antennae are feelers. The spiracles are breathing holes.

One interesting difference between insects and most other animals is the way they are constructed. The animals that we know best generally have hard skeletons inside their bodies. But an insect's skeleton is a protective shield on the outside. This protective "skin" is called an exoskeleton (*exo* means "outside"). This is why the immature insect must molt or shed its skin as it grows. Each new skin is loose enough to allow for more growth. As an insect grows, a new skin is constantly being formed under the old one.

Watching a woolly bear caterpillar shed its skin is a fantastic sight. I watched one once and it took a whole hour. The skin breaks loose around the head and is gradually worked off backwards. As the old skin slowly slips off, each new hair appears to be pulled out of each of the old hairs. It's a slow, tedious job, and at the end of an hour I was as limp and tired as the caterpillar appeared to be. After a short rest, the caterpillar twisted and turned and rolled until all the new wet hairs were dry and fluffy and standing on end. It was a marvelous show and the ticket was free.

Many immature insects do not look at all like their parents. The best way to identify them is to raise them in a jar or terrarium (a large glass container with growing plants). You will need to know whether they eat plants or other insects. You may find out by observing them closely before collecting them.

The ladybug is perhaps the most widely known bug all over the world. But the average person doesn't seem to know what the young, or larva, of a ladybug looks like. It's a tiny, soft-bodied creature with six long legs. It feeds on aphids, the same as its parents. It doesn't change much when it turns into a pupa (the growth stage when an insect is in a hard case). It hangs up by its tail, shrinks in length and swells out into a rounded shape. In about ten days, the back splits open and out crawls a pale whitish ladybug. As you watch, the white slowly changes to color, and black dots begin to appear.

The dragonfly, a graceful creature of the air, spends

A dragonfly nymph climbs out of the water to become an adult (seen at upper left).

the first part of its life at the bottom of a pond or in quiet streams. It's a ferocious creature called a nymph, or in some books, a naiad. Dragonfly nymphs usually take a full year to develop, but sometimes three years or longer, depending on the species. If you are lucky enough to find one that is almost mature, it is interesting to watch. Hunt for one that is about the size of your little finger, or at least one and a half inches long. Examine the back for the well-developed wing cases that show it is nearly grown up. Carry it home in a jar of water and transfer to a large shallow pan or bowl. Add a rock and some sticks, and leave them partly in and partly out of the water. The nymph will need to crawl out of the water when it undergoes its final molt.

Feed it fresh dead flies, small worms, or spiders. If you drop the food where it can be seen, the nymph will snap it up quickly. It takes a keen eye to see its remarkable method of catching food. It has a long underlip that folds back underneath the head. At the end of this lip are a pair of jawlike pincers. The lip flashes in and out like a chameleon's tongue, so rapidly that it is almost impossible to see. The nymph is completely carnivorous and will eat any animal smaller than itself. So do not drop it into your aquarium if you have small fish there. When ready for its final molt, it will crawl out of the water and find a suitable place to fasten its claws. The dark skin splits down the back and a pale, crumpled body slowly works its way out. In several minutes a dazzling dragonfly will be stretching out a pair of brilliant wings.

It's like solving a mystery to watch a small bug grow and shed its skin and finally become an insect you can recognize. If you have katydids in your yard, see if you can find the young ones. They look more like comical little clowns than like their solid, sober parents.

Raising unknown caterpillars is always a challenge. Until a caterpillar reaches its last stage of growth, you can't be sure whether it will be a butterfly or a moth. When it starts to spin a cocoon, you can be fairly sure it will turn into a moth. If it sheds its skin and becomes a chrysalis—a shiny pupa case—you may expect a butterfly. But remember, there are exceptions to every rule and it is these exceptions that make insect study an exciting game.

A beautiful caterpillar of many colors and patterns

does not necessarily mean a beautiful moth or butterfly. And the plainest caterpillar may be an ugly duckling disguising something beautiful. One of the most interesting caterpillars to raise is the tussock, found throughout the United States. You may need to raise this colorful caterpillar, perhaps many of them, to see one of the oddities in the insect world—a wingless female moth. If you find her on a tree, clinging to her cocoon, you will need to be an experienced student to know at once that it is a moth. She has tiny wing pads that move feebly when you touch her. She looks like a part of the fuzzy gray cocoon from which she has emerged. She clings to the outside, mates and lays her eggs there.

Studying, collecting, and raising insects will give you a keen awareness of nature that will stay with you all your life. The purpose of this book is to give you practical details about insects, and suggest ways of getting together with your friends to study them. The following chapters will take up starting a bug club, hunting, raising, and examining insects, bug exhibits, and winter activities for clubs. Grown-ups too may want to help you with a nature club devoted to insect life, so there is a special chapter for them.

Whether you study bugs by yourself or get together with your friends to set up a club—have fun!

Start a Club

$\mathcal{A}$ bug that you find exciting will be twice as interesting if you share your enthusiasm with someone else. It's more fun to work with others than alone.

Tell the boys and girls who live near your home that you are having a bug-club meeting in your back yard Saturday morning at 10 o'clock. Admission is one insect of any kind. Insist on insects and don't consider lizards, snakes, frogs, or other equally interesting creatures. One hour a week is all too short to learn just a little about insects.

Plan to meet at the same place and the same time each week. Keep a record of the members and what they bring. This will give you a growing list of the many different kinds of insects that can be found in your neighborhood. When someone brings a bug that no one knows, that member should try to identify it before the next

In a club, each member can contribute some new bug or bit of knowledge.

meeting. A well illustrated book at your school or public library will help. Don't worry if you can't name all the insects you collect. The best entomologist, or bug expert, in your town may not be able to do this either. You will be doing well if you learn to recognize and name two or three dozen common insects.

It will be helpful to have an adviser to answer some of your questions. Perhaps your school science teacher can suggest a senior 4-H member who is interested in bugs. Or you may find a den mother or a Boy Scout leader who has collected insects. Local museums are generous about answering questions and making suggestions. So are librarians, especially those who work with children and young people.

Let youngsters of any age attend your meetings if they are interested enough to sit and listen. The five-year-old collects his first caterpillar with all the wonderment of the learned scientist discovering a new species. The youngster too young to read can learn a great deal from listening and from looking at pictures.

There was a young boy in our Hayward Library Bug Club in California who knew the pictures as well as the older boys knew the text. One day a seventh-grade boy came in and said, "Look at this bug. He looks like a baby dinosaur." We crowded around, looking and agreeing. None of us had seen it before. As soon as the small boy saw the bug he said, "I know what it is. I know where there's a picture." Our meetings are held in the library, so books are always available. Mac hurried into the adult room and came back with a large book. Turning the pages quickly, he found the picture. There on the page was our baby dinosaur. It was a snakefly. A small black head balanced on the end of an exceedingly long slender neck. We discovered that "dinosaur" is a good name for a snakefly. They are fighters and quickly battle to the death when two or more are confined in a jar.

The way to have a good meeting is to plan in advance just what insects the members will show and talk about, and what club problems you may have to take up, such as raising money for supplies. If someone brings in an insect not on the program, fine—this may lead to even more fun and interest than you had expected. The best meetings are the ones that you keep simple, though. Planning ahead helps to keep them simple.

Working in a club develops a feeling of friendly

competition and a keen desire to do a little bit better than the others. It makes your search more fun to know that you may find something unusual that no one else has found. Also, someone may know just where to hunt for a certain bug that you want in your collection. You can exchange specimens with each other. For two years we hunted in vain for the monarch butterfly caterpillars in the Hayward Library area. No one could find them, although all of us saw numerous monarch butterflies every week. One day a new member came to the bug club with five beautiful green chrysalises. He found the caterpillars near his home. They were in a short two-block area where milkweed was growing along a small drainage ditch.

Some biological-supply houses pay seven to ten cents for winter cocoons. These are the silk-moth cocoons such as the polyphemus, luna, cecropia, promethea, io, and ailanthus. Most of you will find one or more of these in your area. Some of them are found in the woods and others on shade trees along the city streets. Collecting them is an excellent way to raise money for club supplies. Or you may exchange your cocoons for exotic foreign beetles and butterflies.

A common cocoon that is found almost everywhere is the polyphemus. The caterpillar feeds on many trees and shrubs, including birch, which is found in most cities and small towns as well as out in the country. People like to plant birch trees in groups of three in their yards. When you hunt for cocoons in town, *always* go up to the door and ask for permission to look on the trees. Many people

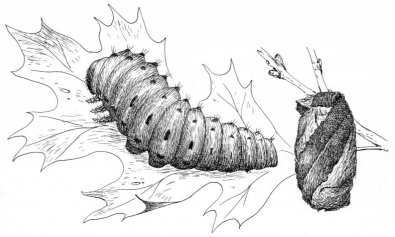

The polyphemus caterpillar and its cocoon

aren't aware of the caterpillars and their cocoons. When you reach for a cocoon, it looks as if you are breaking a branch, and owners don't like this.

Tell them you are working with a science club and are looking for cocoons that should be removed from the trees. Practically everyone will give you permission and, more than that, will come out and hunt with you. They'll go back for a chair to stand on, get a long stick, or bring a ladder if they have one. You will be as amazed as the owners of the trees at the number of cocoons that can be collected in one block. You may come to a yard where the trees are close to the sidewalk and be tempted to reach for a cocoon without asking for permission. But even in this case, don't do it.

Summer is the time when the caterpillars are crawling everywhere. It is also vacation time when the whole family goes away for a trip. Caterpillars need fresh leaves almost every day and it takes an interested person to care for your

caterpillars while you are gone. If a group is working together, this is no problem. You simply exchange "baby-sitting" favors.

Richard, our polyphemus cocoon specialist, did every-thing on a big scale. He called early one morning and said the family was leaving for three days to visit a very ill grandfather. He asked if I would take care of his cater-pillars and cocoons while he was gone. The cocoons might open any hour and he didn't want to leave them at the house. It seemed like a simple request, but Richard had to make three trips to the car to bring in a staggering assortment of jars, terrariums, and plastic bags of fresh food. I took inventory after he left and found:

    10 hungry fritillary caterpillars
      6 huge polyphemus caterpillars
      4 sober tiger swallowtail caterpillars
      4 cecropia cocoons
      4 promethea cocoons
      6 polyphemus cocoons
      3 rubra cocoons

I seriously considered taking three days of my vacation then and there. But I didn't. The caterpillars thrived and all the cocoons remained in deep slumber until Richard returned.

Boys don't have a monoply on insects. Often girls who are interested in collecting them direct this hobby toward future plans. Melinda liked to experiment with her caterpillars and try to change the color and size of her specimens. She liked to explore the inside of an insect by dissecting it. She dreamed of being a veterinarian, an animal doctor. Cathy pinned her butterflies on pieces of driftwood or dried flowers. She used them in original designs as an interior decorator might do.

Working with bugs as a club group will produce widely different viewpoints and brighter ideas in displays. If there are no boys and girls your age near you, invite some of the younger ones to meet with you as their leader. A club can start with only three or four members and then suddenly you will find it growing as if by magic. Try it and see.

Bug Tools

You can have a lot of fun and discover many interesting things about insects with only your eyes and a few hours of time each week. But if you want to make a collection of insects, you will need a few simple aids. In the order of their importance, they are:

> a butterfly net
> a killing jar
> a spreading board
> some insect pins
> a wooden cigar box
> a notebook and sharp pencils
> a *Golden Nature Guide*

Most hobby shops and biological-supply houses carry these items, but the first three are easily made at home. A butterfly net is absolutely necessary if you want a presentable collection of butterflies. Any other method of catching them will either break the fragile wings or spoil the color pattern. The powder on the wings, which produces the beautiful colors and patterns, comes off at the slightest touch.

Butterfly nets are priced from about $1.00 to $3.50. They are quite easy to make at home, as shown in the picture. You will need an old broomstick, a wire coat hanger or piece of heavy wire, and some mosquito netting or an old net curtain. Undo the ends of the coat hanger and twist them closely around the broomstick; then keep them in place by binding them with cord or adhesive tape. Shape the rest into a ring. Make a bag about three feet long with the netting and attach its open end to the ring with thread or bits of fine wire.

After you have collected for a while, you might want a sweeping net. This needs to have a strong frame and the bag made of heavy nylon or light canvas. You sweep this back and forth in tall grass and meadow growth, and across bushes. You will be surprised to see how many interesting bugs you will find in your net. You can sweep at night too and find different kinds of insects.

When you are collecting butterflies, you need a killing jar with you to put them to sleep as quickly and painlessly as possible. Use a wide-mouthed jar with a tight lid. In the bottom, place a small piece of sponge or cotton. Dampen it generously with ethyl acetate, any cleaning fluid, or alcohol. In an emergency, fingernail-polish remover can be used. (Some collectors use cyanide,

It isn't hard to make a butterfly net.

but this is such a dangerous poison that it should be avoided.) Over the wet cotton, place a circle of aluminum foil or wax paper. A crumpled facial tissue dropped in will prevent butterflies from injuring their wings.

Someone may ask how you can bear to kill a beautiful butterfly. This bothered me until I talked to an experienced entomologist. He told me that butterflies meet death in several ways. If they live out their normal lives, they usually drop to the ground and ants eat them while they are still alive. Or they may be caught by birds, which can also be a lingering death. Being put to sleep in a killing jar is a more merciful death than these.

It's not wise to put beetles in a killing jar at the same time as butterflies. Their sharp claws may damage the butterfly wings. Also, the scales from the wings may rub off on the beetles. For beetles (but never for flies or bees) it's better to carry a separate jar with alcohol in it. Rubbing alcohol will do; avoid wood alcohol (also called methanol), which can harm the skin. You might not want to carry a butterfly net in a large city, but you can carry a small jar of alcohol. I carried one at all hours in Mexico City and picked up some fascinating beetles from window-sills and doorways.

A spreading board will be needed to make winged insects like moths, butterflies, and dragonflies dry with their wings properly outspread. It consists of two long boards of soft balsa wood mounted side by side, with a space between them to allow room for the insect's body. If they are not made of balsa, they can be topped with cork or corrugated cardboard so that pins can be pushed into them. Each board slopes slightly upward toward its outer side.

A local Boy Scout troop might plan a project of making boards for the club. A start can be made with one board, and it can be loaned each week to a different member until all have their own boards. Layers of corrugated cardboard can be a temporary substitute.

It will take a bit of practice before you can mount a butterfly easily and properly. One tiny slip and a wing tears; an awkward movement and an antenna snaps off. You will want the specimens you keep to be as nearly perfect as possible. Practice on the small white cabbage butterflies, which are an agricultural pest. Each member will probably develop his own technique of mounting. By watching others you may find a better way than your own.

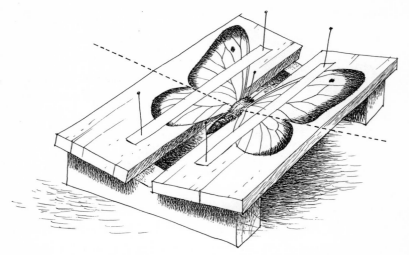

This is the way a butterfly is mounted on the spreading board. The lower edges of the front wings should line up with each other, as shown by the dotted line.

Place the body of your pinned butterfly in the groove of the spreading board with the wings resting flat on the sides of it. Slide the front wings forward until their lower edges make a straight line with each other across the board. The hind wings should be adjusted until they barely slide under the edges of the front ones. Hold all the wings by pinning strips of paper over them. In the wings there are strong veins behind which you can carefully insert a pin to push them into position. Most butterflies will dry in two or three days. The large moths may take a week. If you remove them from the board too soon, the wings will slip or droop.

Special insect pins are necessary if you want to keep a collection. Common pins will rust and spoil your speci-

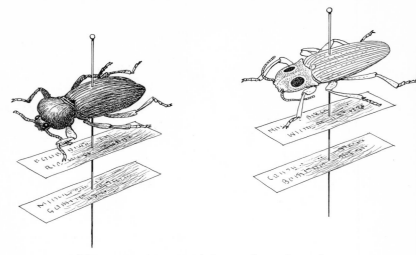

Mount your insect straight, neatly, and evenly.

mens. They are too large and thick for insects. Insect pins are thin and strong and will not rust. They cost about seventy-five cents for a package of a hundred. They come in several sizes; number three is a good size to start with. Only one pin should be used for each specimen; the paper strips can be held in place with common pins. For a start, the club could buy one package of pins and let each member buy eight or ten. Pins can be bought from biological-supply houses. There is a list of them at the end of this book.

Most of the insects that you collect will not need a special preservative. The soft inside parts dry up and the outside keeps its original appearance. Caterpillars and other larvas should be preserved in small vials of 70 per cent alcohol or a 5 per cent solution of formaldehyde. Many soft-bodied adult insects, such as silverfish, spring-tails, stoneflies, and termites, also should be preserved in

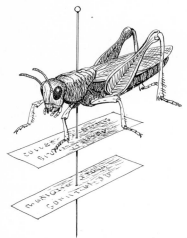

fluid. Label each vial, giving the insect's name, locality, plant food, and date.

Once your specimens are pinned and dried, you will need a special container for them. Large redwood boxes can be purchased from supply houses, but wooden cigar boxes are excellent too. Maybe a friendly storekeeper will save an empty one for you. Cut a piece of cardboard or styrofoam to fit the bottom of the box tightly. This will make it easier to pin your specimens firmly so they won't fall over. Cigar boxes made of cardboard can be used too, but they lack the tight lids of the wooden boxes. There are tiny mites and museum beetles that will find your insects and destroy the whole collection. A constantly renewed supply of moth flakes will help repel the invaders.

A small label should tell where each specimen was collected, date of collecting, and the collector's name. A second label, to be placed lower on the pin, gives the insect's name. The labels should be on good-quality, fairly heavy paper so they will stay flat when cut out and not slip on the pin. Use a fine pen and print as small as possible. All the specimens should be at the same height (and the labels a little lower, likewise at one height) to give your collection a professional appearance.

Some insects are pinned through the center of the thorax, others to the right of the center. Insects too small to pin should be mounted on slender triangles of paper. These triangles are pinned through the wide end and the specimen is attached to the very tip—preferably with white shellac or a cement like Duco. Be careful to use just a tiny touch of the adhesive.

You may want to frame some of your specimens in a Riker mount. This is a flat cardboard box filled with cotton and covered with a glass top. These can be freely handled without injury to the specimens and can be purchased from most supply houses.

There is an excellent series of books called the *Golden Nature Guides.* Each book combines the knowledge of an eminent scientist and of an expert in science education, Dr. Herbert S. Zim. The books can be purchased in paperback editions in many drug stores and stationery stores for one dollar each. Two of the *Guides* seem made to order for bug clubs:

Insects, by Herbert S. Zim and Clarence Cottam, contains excellent full-color illustrations of 225 common insects found throughout the United States.

Butterflies and Moths, by Robert T. Mitchell and Herbert S. Zim, contains 423 full-color illustrations of butterflies and moths, their caterpillars, eggs, chrysalises, and cocoons.

If you can buy only one book, start with *Insects.* It covers a wide variety of butterflies and moths, beetles, true bugs, dragonflies, wasps, ants, and other orders. It

would be an excellent idea for a club to raise two dollars and buy one copy of each book for club use at the meetings. Most of you will want a personal copy of one or the other, once you have looked at them.

An item that is not necessary but will give you a great deal of pleasure is a small magnifying glass. Under a magnifying glass, the speck of a butterfly egg turns into a neat little barrel with ridges running up and down, or it may look like a flat pancake with brown edges. Examine other insect eggs and see how each type varies in design and pattern. Some eggs are laid singly and others in groups. It will give you a real feeling of accomplishment to find insect eggs and recognize them by name, as a tiger swallowtail egg or a ladybug egg.

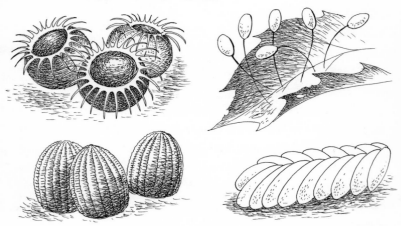

Insect eggs take all kinds of shapes. At the upper left are stinkbug eggs; at upper right, lacewing. The three that look like cactuses are butterfly eggs, and the mass of eggs together is from a grass-hopper.

The most interesting eggs to hunt for are those of the green lacewing. Sometimes they are underneath a leaf and other times on top, often ten or twelve close together. Each tiny white egg is fastened on the tip of a fine thread-like stalk that sways in the breeze. When the eggs hatch, the tiny creatures that come out haven't the faintest resemblance to the green lacewing. They are a smaller and softer version of the ladybug larvas. Let one crawl on your finger and watch it through your magnifying glass. It has a pair of tiny sharp pincers that it will try to fasten into your tough skin. You can barely feel it, but minutes later that spot will redden and begin to itch. This is a bare beginning of the tiny things you ordinarily miss in nature. A magnifying glass can open a whole new world to you.

Good Hunting!

No matter where you live, in the country on a farm, or in the city in an apartment, there are insects somewhere near you.

Your yard may be small and look empty but it can be full of surprises. Stand quietly near some bushes or flowers and use your eyes. A bit of movement and you may see an inchworm "measuring" a flower stem. Out of the air a butterfly floats down to sip from a blossom. At your feet a black beetle hurries along and out of sight. Across the toe of your shoe scurry a few curious ants.

Is there a board near a garden faucet? Turn it over and see how many small creatures burst into action. Some of them are not insects. There may be sowbugs and snails and slugs. Leave them and catch the beetles and earwigs before they disappear. Then put the board back where it was so you will have the fun of looking again. There might be something different another time. Always replace a log or stone you turn over.

If you go outdoors on a warm summer evening and listen, you will hear the cheerful singing and chirping of katydids and crickets. Usually it is the male who sings to attract a female. Have you ever watched one when it is rubbing its wings together? With a flashlight you can trace these odd night sounds to their source. If you're quiet, the light doesn't seem to bother them and they will continue to perform for you. The angular-winged katydid makes a peculiar squeaking sound that is difficult to describe. Once you have seen the katydid you will recognize his voice and he will become a special friend.

One of the loveliest of the night singers to watch is the snowy tree cricket. It's a small, delicate insect found on trees, also on low bushes and plants. In my yard they are on both the lemon tree and the geraniums. The wings of the snowy tree cricket are green but so pale and transparent that they appear to be white. The male is often visible at the edge of a leaf with his wings lifted high and spread over his back. You can usually find the female on an adjoining leaf. She has wings but holds them close to her body. She lays her eggs in the stems of plants and can become a pest. Put a male and a female in a jar and they will sing for you in the house—in fact, at all hours of the night. They will eat from a slice of cucumber, a crumbled bit of cookie or dog biscuit.

Many of you live where you have a shrill and strident singer in the daytime. The hotter the day, the louder the

A cicada climbs out of its exoskeleton, leaving a perfect but empty model of itself behind.

song, until it almost hurts your ears. This is the cicada, often incorrectly called a locust. The song—if you can call it a song—is really a shrill drumming sound. The male cicada has an odd circular plate near the base of each wing. The noise is made by rapidly tightening and relaxing special muscles. These drum plates are raised and lowered to increase or soften the sound. A female doesn't have a drum; she does have a sharp ovipositor, or egg-laying organ, with which she slices small openings in the twigs of trees, and in these slits she lays her eggs. When the eggs hatch, the small, pale nymphs drop to the ground and burrow underneath. They feed on the sap of roots. Some species live underground for one year and others as long as seventeen or even twenty years.

The seventeen-year "locust" has been known in America since 1633. These insects have been carefully studied by scientists for a long time, and still put on an amazing and surprising performance. One group, known as No. X, came out of the ground in 1953. In 1970 scientists from all over the country will gather to watch the new ones come out. They never appear in sixteen years, or in eighteen, but always in seventeen.

They come swarming out of the ground, crawl up the nearest tree trunks and dig in with their claws. Their shells, or exoskeletons, split open on the back and out climb colorful winged creatures. They beat their drums fast and furiously, almost as though they knew that their life above ground lasts only a few days.

In the warmer parts of the country you can hunt for insects every month of the year. Where there are cold winters, late spring and summer are the best times for collecting. The ideal time of day is between 10 A.M. and 2 P.M. Warm, sunny days are better than cool or windy days. Early evening is the time to hunt for moths, crickets and a few other insects. A porch light will attract many interesting fliers and often strange visitors will appear on the outside of the windowpanes of a well-lighted room.

The most exciting places to hunt for bugs are in the open fields, along the banks of ponds and streams, along the roadsides, under rotten logs, and beneath loose bark of trees.

Some of the easiest insects for beginners to collect are beetles, ants, and dragonflies. These bugs are easy to handle, easy to pin, and do not come apart as quickly and unexpectedly as butterflies do. There are thousands of

beetles, and beetles are found everywhere. Look under loose boards and stones, under bark, in the grass, on bushes or trees, around rotten stumps and old logs. Many small ones will be in your flower garden. When collecting beetles, the easiest way to kill them is to drop them into a small jar partly full of alcohol. Remember, don't drop beetles into a killing jar with butterflies. You may ruin both specimens this way.

Do you know how many different kinds of flies you can collect? In your yard and an open field nearby you might find a housefly, a horsefly, a tachinid fly, a bee fly, a syrphid fly, tiny fruit flies, and an ichneumon fly. There are many more, but these are the common ones.

The best time to hunt for butterflies is during the middle of a warm day. You will not see many on a cool, cloudy day or in windy periods. An open field full of weeds and wildflowers is an excellent place to start, as is a meadow with a small stream running through it. And even if you have few flowers in your yard, a butterfly may pass through on its way to some other place and provide you with an exciting specimen.

It may take a little practice to catch the butterfly you want. If you run after a butterfly you may frighten it away. If you swoop and miss, it may zoom up high and disappear. Watch a butterfly and walk toward it slowly when it is feeding on a flower. When you are close, swoop quickly with your net, then twist the handle so the bag folds over the opening. It's amazing how easily a butterfly can escape when you think it is safely in the bag. Some butterflies will drop to the ground and slip out under the edge of your net. Or they will hide quietly in the grass until you raise your net, then zip unexpectedly past your nose. Each effort will teach you how to do it better next time. Always be careful to handle the net gently to avoid damaging your specimen.

In collecting butterflies, look at your catch before putting it in your killing jar. If it is damaged or worn by age, turn it loose and look for another one. A collection to keep or show should be as nearly perfect as possible. And when you are setting your specimens, be careful not to break the fragile antennae.

If you cannot mount and pin your butterflies the same day you catch them, you will need to use a relaxing jar. You can use any type of container with a close-fitting lid. I find a one-pound coffee can excellent, as I don't like to relax too many specimens at one time. Place a folded paper towel in the can and dampen it thoroughly to create a moist atmosphere. A teaspoon or so of moth flakes must be added to prevent mold. Place your insects on a piece of wax paper or something to keep them off the wet towel. Leave them inside for from twelve to thirty-six hours. Test them carefully to see if all parts will move easily. Then they are ready for the spreading board.

Moths are not so easy to find and catch because they come out of hiding after dark. The eastern and southern parts of our country have six or more of the big exciting silk moths. The club, or two or three of you, should plan an evening with moth bait. An easy bait can be made from

several overripe bananas mashed with a generous amount of brown sugar. Let this mixture stand for a few hours; it should be thick but easy to spread. The sweeter it is and the stronger it smells, the better. Late in the afternoon is the time to do your "sugaring." Trees on the edge of a woods or in a wooded area are the best ones to select. Pick the ones you can find again after dark. Fence posts are good, too, if there are trees nearby. Smear generous amounts of the banana-sugar on the tree trunks or fence posts about ten or twelve feet apart.

The warm evening of a hot day will produce the most moths. And it will be better if there is no moon. Take a flashlight and your killing jar when you go back after dark to investigate. Be quiet as you turn your light on the first tree. If you are lucky, it will be an exciting sight. Pick out the specimen you want first. Take the lid off your killing jar and, placing the jar directly under the moth, bring it up. The moth is more likely to drop than to fly away. Make the rounds of all your spots and, if you aren't lucky tonight, try again tomorrow night. Take a look at the sugared spots during the day, too. Butterflies and other insects will be attracted to the sweetness.

Another baiting method is especially good for collecting beetles and other small bugs. These are jar traps that are buried in the ground with the open top even with the surface. Some bugs are attracted to sweet food and others to decaying meat. Experiment with both kinds of bait in different areas of your yard. A loose board or stone over the edge of the jar will make the spot inviting.

A small notebook that will slip into a pocket and a couple of short (and sharp) pencil stubs should be a part of your equipment at all times. It takes no more than a minute to jot down the name of your specimen, the date, time of day, place and weather conditions:

> Tiger Swallowtail
> June 10 [plus year and time of day]
> Near willow tree in park
> Warm, sunny day

This may not seem necessary at first, but you'll be glad later on that you did it. The entry above will tell you a year later where to look for a tiger swallowtail, and also where to hunt for eggs and chrysalises. In a few years you will be the author of a personal field guide of your home area. Here is a sample from a notebook:

May 10, 1964—sunny day
West Coast lady caterpillar on mallow in driveway.
Tiger swallowtail flew through yard—10 A.M.
Two mourning cloaks chasing each other in grape arbor—10 A.M.

May 25—warm, slight breeze
Anise swallowtail laying eggs on anise near schoolhouse—10 A.M.
Buckeye—field near schoolhouse—10 A.M.
Monarch—near neighbor's back fence—2 P.M.
Gulf fritillary on passion vine near Macy's—3 P.M.

June 20—all-day picnic at Marsh Creek—very warm

Two-tailed swallowtails	Buckeyes
Western tailed blues	Robber flies
Chalcedon checkerspots	Bee flies
Caddis-fly larva	Dragonflies
Giant crane fly	Mud daubers

To identify the insects you find, you will need a book or two. A good book on insects for beginners should be generously illustrated. Go through such a book two or three times examining the pictures. You may not find a picture *exactly* like your specimen, but you should find one that looks like the *type* of insect you have. Examine your specimen closely. Does it have two or four wings? Does it have a long sucking tube or strong jaws for biting? If it looks like a beetle, does it have a V-shaped wedge on its back? These observations will help you to identify your specimen as a beetle, a fly, true bug, a wasp, etc. Butterflies and moths will be difficult to identify without a picture in front of you and, if possible, in color. The two *Golden Nature Guides* mentioned in the "bug tools"

The rather rare dobsonfly has a short life.

chapter are excellent. Other titles are named at the end of this book.

When you find an insect that is completely new and strange to you, it is a thrill to imagine that you have found something rare. Never overlook the possibility that it may be just that. One of the boys in our club found a large dark brown moth on the street, the wing edges badly frayed. We identified it as the black witch, a tropical moth that may have flown all the way from Mexico. This moth is not exactly rare, but to find one is unusual. Therefore it becomes a rare specimen for the finder.

Insects aren't the only things to gather. You will find that collecting skin molts, face masks (molts of the eyes and facial parts), empty chrysalises and cocoons, wasps' paper "apartment houses" (empty!), mud daubers' cells, and other such things is almost as fascinating as finding the bugs themselves. And a collection of insect eggs can be mounted on microscope slides for use with a hand lens or a low-power microscope. Kill them in the killing jar, let them dry thoroughly if they seem moist, and then mount them in balsam or some other mounting fluid intended for slides; or else use simply hot paraffin for your eggs.

Raise Your Own Bugs

Not all people who are interested in insects make a collection. Some like to raise caterpillars and watch them grow and change. Try it once, and every spring you'll find yourself doing it again and again. It's fun to watch a caterpillar's sturdy mouth devour a leaf as fast and effectively as a small lawn mower. Next to birds, insects are perhaps the most colorful and fascinating of all creatures.

A caterpillar could be your first pet. It is yours for the finding and costs nothing but the little time and effort it takes to care for it. The only space required for this pet is enough room for a wide-mouthed jar or a small screened box. If you care for your caterpillar correctly, there should be no objections from other members of your family.

With a little experience you can find and raise all the

different kinds of caterpillars in your neighborhood. This may seem difficult at first, but after you have found a few, you will learn how to look for others. Some caterpillars feed on the under side of a leaf, others on top. The tiger swallowtail weaves a small platform on a leaf where it rests, but wanders a foot or more away to do its eating. There are some caterpillars that rest between two leaves so cleverly fastened together that it takes a knowing eye to find their hiding place. To hunt on the leaves that look chewed is useless—you'll find nothing.

A weeping willow tree is a regular apartment house for caterpillars. During July we can usually find at least seven different kinds on our willow: puss moth, mourning cloak, polyphemus (a bit unusual), Lorquin's admiral, twin-spotted sphinx, yellow woolly bear, and the arctiid moth.

The secret of raising caterpillars is to have a fresh supply of leaves practically every day. The leaves must be from the same tree or plant on which you found your caterpillar. Most caterpillars will not change from one kind of plant to another for their food. If you find one wandering along on the ground, the chances are that it is hunting for a place to spin its cocoon or make its chrysalis. Caterpillars seldom leave the plant on which they are feeding unless they are disturbed in some accidental way.

If you find a caterpillar in some odd place away from food, and it appears still to have an appetite, you may have a real mystery to solve. If you can't find the right food

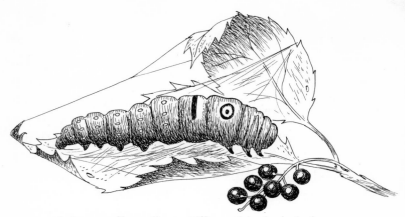

A tiger swallowtail caterpillar and its leaf platform

plant, your developing insect may die before it will change to a new kind. Collect different kinds of leaves in the area where you found the specimen. Put three or four in the jar with it and watch. If it crawls over them and keeps going in circles, you know you haven't found the right food plant. Take the leaves out and put in some different ones. As soon as you put the right leaves in, the caterpillar will settle and start nibbling.

Until you have a good deal of experience, it isn't wise to raise more than two or three caterpillars at one time. They require more attention and food than you may suspect. We made this mistake in the early days of the Bug Club at Hayward. We heard that we could find pipe-vine swallowtails at a place about thirty miles away. We found a vine growing along a small stream, abundantly covered with these startling blue-black creatures with orange dots and fleshy horns. I cautioned the boys to collect only the largest ones, and not too many. It would be a long way back for food.

In spite of my warning, we overdid it. In a week we were all out of food and the caterpillars were still eating ravenously. As they grew in size, their appetites became enormous. Leaves and stems and buds disappeared as fast as we could supply them. First one, then a second boy had to persuade his father to drive the sixty-mile round trip for more food. Many adults, you may discover, are not enthusiastic about driving long distances to get food for "those worms."

It was at this time that we learned about "cannibals." One of the boys ran out of food several days before the fresh supply came. When he looked at his caterpillars one morning, he found them eating fresh chrysalises. Sometimes hungry caterpillars will eat each other. So collect plenty of food when you are gathering them away from home. Put the extra food in a plastic bag with just a light sprinkle of water and ask if you may keep it in the refrigerator. Most plant food will stay fresh this way for a week or ten days.

In the warmer parts of our country, a few caterpillars can be found the year round. Many of you will have to hunt for them in the spring or early summer. Carry your caterpillar home on the leaf or twig on which you find it. Place it in a wide-mouthed jar and cover the top with a piece of net or old nylon stocking held in place by a rubber band. Keep the jar dry and clean and emptied of droppings each day.

The leaves or twigs must be fresh and not wilted, so place two or three small stems of food in a small pill

A caterpillar jar should be clean, dry, and safe.

bottle of water. If the bottle can tip easily, fasten it in the jar with adhesive tape. Cover the top of the pill bottle with cotton or paper. Caterpillars have an odd habit of crawling down into the water and drowning. If you find a caterpillar in the water, remove it very carefully and place it on a paper towel or a large leaf. It may appear to be dead, but wait an hour or more. They often revive and then start eating again quite as though nothing had happened.

When you put fresh food in the jar, leave the caterpillar on the old stems and let it crawl onto the new ones. Your growing larva may be getting ready to shed its old skin and should not be disturbed at this time. A caterpillar molts four or five times to allow for more growth.

One day your caterpillar will stop eating and crawl restlessly around the jar. It is looking for a place to hang its chrysalis or spin its cocoon. Avoid handling it at this time. If it is a butterfly caterpillar, watch and see if you can catch the exciting moment when the larva's old skin splits to reveal a completely new shape and color, the pupa or chrysalis.

I hope all of you will have the experience of watching a monarch caterpillar make this change. The chrysalis has been forming under the skin. As the skin splits and rolls off, the feet and the head disappear with it, leaving a shapeless, colorless blob of a chrysalis. But within a few minutes something that seems like a miracle occurs. As the chrysalis dries, it takes on a solid, plump shape and turns a clear green. Then a row of shiny gold dots forms a half

circle near the top and a few scattered gold dots decorate the bottom area, and we have a jewel of jade and gold.

The monarch chrysalis opens in seven or eight days. If you want to watch a butterfly emerge from its chrysalis, the monarch is one of the best for the experiment. When the orange and black wing pattern shows clearly through the thin shell, remove the chrysalis from the jar and place it in direct warm sunshine. It should open in five or ten minutes. You will hear a thin *pop!* like the breaking of a miniature paper bag. Two long black feet reach out and fasten on the outside of the shell, the antennae flip out, then the limp, wet body and crumpled wings appear. The butterfly starts pumping liquid from its heavy body into the veins in its wings. As the veins become full, the wings stretch out to their full size. They are fanned slowly back and forth until they are dry. The tongue, which comes in two pieces, is constantly curled and uncurled until it zips together, forming a tube for sucking nectar from flowers. If you are outdoors in the sun, your monarch will make a trial flight almost any minute.

Most butterflies are excitable and will flutter wildly when confined. But a monarch that you have raised, not captured, is a butterfly that you can keep as a pet. It will be content in a house sitting on a plant in a sunny window. Two or three times a day, put a drop of sugar and water, or honey and water, in the palm of your hand and offer it. The monarch will stand on your hand, uncurl its long tongue and sip the sweetness. It's fun to do this for a few days; then let your butterfly go free.

Sometimes tragedy strikes unexpectedly. One morning you may notice a tiny hole in your lovely green chrysalis, and in about two hours the soft green color is gone, leaving only the bright shiny gold dots. Keep the jar covered. In a week the chrysalis will be dark gray, with a few black spots here and there. At the end of the second week, a tachinid fly may hatch from a small red pupa that you probably noticed in the bottom of the jar and you will have a new specimen for your collection. Caterpillars are often killed by parasites, as this one was, by having eggs laid on them.

If you are raising a moth caterpillar, it will either spin a cocoon or go down into the dirt to change into a pupa. If it continues circling the jar restlessly, put three or four inches of moist dirt in a container such as a coffee can, place your caterpillar on the dirt, and watch. If you have waited a little too long, it may dive into the dirt and disappear before your eyes. If this is early summer, the moth may come out soon. Wait about ten days, then gently shake the dirt out of the can until you find the pupa. Place it on a damp blotter in the breeding cage. Have several sturdy twigs in the cage so the moth will have something to cling to when it comes out of its shell.

If you have cocoons and chrysalises to keep for the winter, they will need special care if they are to remain alive and healthy. Place them in clean cans with tight covers. Store the cans in the garage or in a cupboard on the back porch and leave them until spring. The pupas will not dry out and beetles and mice cannot attack them.

With a little practice, you can tell if your cocoon is alive. A cocoon with a live pupa has weight, but one in which the pupa is dead feels as light as a piece of paper. Also, many live pupas will move around when disturbed, causing the cocoons to shake vigorously. But not all of them will do this. One cocoon may rustle and wiggle every day and another beside it may not, yet both may be alive. This is another "exception to the rule."

When the trees start to leaf out, take your cocoons and chrysalises out of the cans and put them in a properly prepared cage or terrarium. Place them on damp moss or a dampened blotter, and watch every day for signs of opening. With a little experience, you can tell when a pupa or chrysalis is about to open by its swollen and stretched appearance.

Some chrysalises of the same species will open in two weeks, or be delayed two months or even two years. The anise and the tiger swallowtails are like this. Sometimes a chrysalis will become stiff and hard from a parasite and will never produce a butterfly. If you are in doubt about your chrysalis, touch it gently. If the small end is movable, it is alive. If it is as stiff as a stick, it is dead; cut it open and examine it.

In reading about insects and their behavior, keep in mind the exceptions to the rule. Insects in captivity may not follow the same pattern as when they are free outdoors. There is a book that says "polyphemus cocoons always open early in the morning." Perhaps nature arranged it this way and allowed their wings to dry and harden before the evening, when they start flying. But the first polyphemus moth I saw emerge came from its cocoon at 5:30 in the evening.

Such differences are the things that excite the curiosity of a scientist. Why does one chrysalis turn yellow and the one beside it green? Why do six tiny caterpillars start nibbling on a walnut leaf while three wander off and settle for sweet gum? Why don't you try to find out some of the answers? You might discover something that no one has found out before.

A praying mantis is perhaps the most fascinating insect pet. It is the only insect that turns its head and looks at you and appears to respond when you speak to it. Once you have had one, you will want one every year. If they are native to your area, let them grow up outdoors and collect an adult in August.

The first time you put out your hand and let a mantis walk onto it, it acts like a friend. It will stand high on four legs and wave the two front legs in the air as though asking to be picked up. It will turn its head from side to side as you move. One pet will be all you want. You can't keep two together, as one may eat the other. And a grown mantis has a huge appetite. In one day I fed one three grasshoppers, two katydids, four flies, three skippers, and two inchworms. And the mantis wants these alive.

When you keep a mantis indoors, it will live longer than it would outdoors. In fact, it will live longer than the supply of fresh insects. Your mantis will learn to eat

Adult mantis, baby, and egg case

readily from your fingers or from a toothpick. It will enjoy small bits of fresh liver as much as a juicy grasshopper. Hamburger is a bit dry and not so appetizing. It will also drink from a teaspoon. Amuse your friends by offering it a few drops of milk from a spoon. It likes juicy fruit, especially watermelon. And watch afterwards as it carefully cleans its feet and face.

Be prepared to lose your mantis in a fairly short time. The average life for many mantises is five or six months. When hand fed, they will often live two or three months longer. One day your mantis will refuse to eat. It has reached the end of its life span. And you can start planning to have another one next summer.

If you buy an egg case, be sure to keep it in the garage or some equally cool place until spring. You won't want the mantises to hatch until your garden or nearby weeds have a plentiful supply of aphids. The tiny mantises will eat aphids for about six weeks, then larger insects.

Another method is to fasten your egg case outside to a plant that will not be sprayed or trimmed. Berry vines make an excellent mantis nursery. When the weather becomes warm, look at the egg case each day and you will be able to pick up two or three mantises the day they hatch. Leave the others to take care of themselves and hunt for adults about two months later. If they have plenty of aphids, two or three infants can live together while small, but in captivity things seem to go wrong when they are trying to molt. Give them something more roomy and airy than a jar.

When you have an adult female mantis, you may have the interesting experience of watching her make an egg case. It's a long, tedious job and takes her about an hour. Mantises usually make two or three egg cases and each one holds about two hundred eggs.

When raising insects, keep a record of your observations during the life cycle. Records are interesting to read and compare because of their variations. This is part of the record that one of the boys in the club made:

July 26. Found 3 small, round cream-colored eggs on elm tree.

Aug. 9. All 3 hatched about 8 A.M. Tiny spiny cater-pillars with large heads. 2 ate most of egg shells, one did not. . . .

Sept. 24. 2 are pulling leaves together with a fine silk web.

Sept. 25. Third started cocoon this morning.

Sept. 28. Silvery cocoons have turned dark brown and are firm. Put in coffee can in garage.

March 15. Brought cocoons into my room. Fastened 2 on window curtains, took one to school.

March 25. Cocoons rattle and rustle—feel alive in my hand.

April 10. After school found beautiful big female polyphemus hanging quietly from one of the cocoons.

April 11. Took polyphemus to school.

April 12. Polyphemus is laying eggs all over the place.

April 13. Can hardly count the eggs—must be over 100.

April 14. Teacher mounted polyphemus for school collection.

April 24. 2 remaining cocoons both noisy but nothing happens.

April 28. Cocoon at school opened over the weekend. Can't find moth anywhere.

May 20. My second cocoon opened and I missed it again. Will raise at least six this summer. Maybe I can catch one coming out.

There are many other life cycles to watch. Crickets, katydids, and grasshoppers go through a three-stage cycle called an incomplete metamorphosis, meaning that they are born and grow up looking much like adults. The young insects are called nymphs instead of larvas. The main change in growth is to acquire wings like the adults.

Grasshoppers are easy to raise; they thrive on a diet of fresh grass every day. You should raise them once to watch them shed their skins. They will molt five or six times. Each time you will notice that the abdomen is a little larger, the legs a little longer. In the third week tiny wing pads appear. In about seven weeks the last molt occurs and the full wings develop. The underwings, which show only in flight, are often brightly colored.

When you are collecting in the field, watch the grasshoppers as they fly up in front of you. Some will show a flash of red, some yellow and some blue. In mounting grasshoppers for a collection, open one wing to show the color.

Most beetles are difficult to raise because it is almost impossible to construct a natural habitat for the larvas. Many of the larvas live underground or in tree trunks. Some of them take two or three years to develop into adults. You may keep the larger or more colorful ones alive for a few days in a terrarium. Most of them will eat bits of meat, lettuce, fruit, or vegetables.

If you are interested in water insects, you may plan and stock an insect aquarium. If you want many kinds of

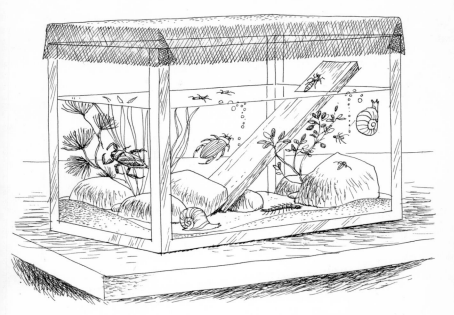

Water insects in a properly made aquarium can put on a fascinating show.

insects, you will need several aquariums to keep the larger ones from eating the smaller ones. A rectangular glass aquarium is best for watching underwater activity.

A quiet stream or small pond is a good collecting place. You need a basket in which to carry three or four empty jars and a water net. This net is smaller and stronger than your butterfly net. The handle is shorter, the net of heavier material and shaped like half a grapefruit rather than a cone.

You will need an inch or two of clean sand for the bottom of your aquarium. To be sure the sand is free of germs or fungi, either buy it at a pet shop or bake it in a hot oven for about one hour. Fill your aquarium about two-thirds full of water. Place in it several green plants for food and to keep the water supplied with oxygen. Watercress will be especially good for your vegetarian insects, also elodea and other small plants from the pond. Use a few stones to anchor your plants on the bottom. Also add some slanting sticks that extend above the water surface on which the larvas and nymphs may crawl when ready for their final molt. Keep your aquarium clean. A snail or two will take care of the green algae that form on the sides. And a small catfish is a good scavenger on the bottom. The aquarium will need light, but avoid direct sunlight.

Some water insects are carnivores—animal-eaters—and others are vegetarians, or plant-eaters. You must learn to know them and keep them in separate quarters if you want the vegetarians to survive. The carnivorous ones will need small insects, like mosquito larvas, for food. They also accept tiny bits of fresh meat. Some of the insects that you can bring home from the pond are dragon-fly naiads, caddis fly larvas, water-boatmen, backswimmers, water striders, both stonefly and mayfly nymphs, and whirligig beetles. You will need wire screening to cover and extend the height of your aquarium. This will prevent the new adult insects from flying away before you see them.

When Winter Comes

*C*hilly weather may come and insects may seem to disappear, but there are still many things to do in a bug club. Spend some time improving the physical appearance of your collection. Examine each specimen and see that it is correctly labeled. Try to identify the insects you haven't named yet. Search through books, compare notes with other members; if possible, visit a local nature museum.

When the trees are bare of leaves, cocoons are easily spotted hanging from the branches. Go collecting with a pocket knife, a paper bag and your notebook and pencil. If you know the food plant of the moths, it will make your search much easier. You will need to know the trees and shrubs and how to recognize them in their winter bareness. Look for cynthia cocoons on the ailanthus tree, polyphemus on birch and elm, promethea on wild cherry and sassafras, luna on hickory and persimmon.

Sphinx-moth pupas (below) *can be dug up around tomato plants.*

Some cocoons, like the luna, are spun on the ground. To find them, you must search carefully among the leaves under the trees. Other moth caterpillars pupate, or go through their pupa stage, in the ground. Dig gently around the base of trees or shrubs that might have had caterpillars during the summer. Dig around tomato plants for the "little brown jug with the handle," the pupa of the sphinx moth. These pupas can be stored in covered coffee cans until spring.

The easiest cocoons to find will be those hanging from the branches of trees. If there is a particular species  you want that pupates in the ground, you should try to find the caterpillar and raise it. In collecting cocoons, break or cut the twig with the cocoon intact. It is easier to keep a cocoon if it is left on a twig six or eight inches long. When the moth emerges, it will be in position to hang its wings down to dry and harden.

Enter in your notebook the date, the name of the cocoon, the plant food it was on, and where it was found. Store your cocoons in covered containers in the garage or some other cool place. *Never* be tempted to drop two or three cocoons into a dresser drawer thinking you will take care of them later. It is easy to forget about them and, in the warmth of your room, they will open early. One day your mother may open that dresser drawer and nearly faint as a big, furry monster flies into her face. And it isn't a good way to establish insect relations with your family.

Dissecting an insect is a stimulating project for the older members. A large grasshopper is an easy insect to handle. Grasshoppers should be collected during the summer and preserved in a bottle of alcohol. You will need a hand lens, small scissors with fine, straight blades, a single-edge razor blade, a piece of cardboard about 8 × 10 inches and a tube of glue.

As you remove the parts, arrange and fasten them on the cardboard with a spot of glue. Label each part as you remove it. This will give each member an opportunity to examine the parts with the hand lens and some may want to make drawings of them.

Examine your specimen and locate the three main body divisions: the head, the thorax and the abdomen. The wings and the legs are attached to the thorax and we will begin with this section. Remove the wings and glue one pair to the cardboard. Snip off the legs and keep three from the same side. All the legs have the same number of segments, the main ones being the femur, tibia, and tarsus, ending with a pair of tarsal claws.

On the head, locate the antennae or feelers, two compound eyes (the large ones, with a silky-looking surface), three simple eyes, and the mouth parts. Before cutting, examine the mouth closely with your hand lens. Carefully remove the upper lip (labrum) and behind it the jaws (mandibles). There is a lower lip (labium) and behind it the tongue (hypopharynx). Notice that the grasshopper chews sideways instead of up and down.

Dissecting the insides of an insect is a delicate job likely to require additional instruments (a couple of large needles are often helpful). Work slowly and carefully so you don't destroy an organ before you know it is there. You will find just under the back a long tubelike blood vessel, and a swelling in it that is the heart. There is a food canal and a reproductive system. Also a small brain and nerve cord that runs along the lower part of the body. Insect blood is usually colorless, pale yellow, or greenish. Since there are no arteries and veins, it flows freely through the body cavity. There are no lungs for breathing. Along each side of the body there is a row of breathing holes or spiracles. Tiny tubes carry the air directly from the spiracle openings to all parts of the body.

Examine several grasshoppers and notice the difference in the hind or caudal end of the body. The female has a tapered abdomen ending with four pointed and horny pieces. The male's abdomen ends with a single large, hood-shaped plate.

When you have mastered the grasshopper project, try a large katydid or Jerusalem cricket and see what you can discover on your own.

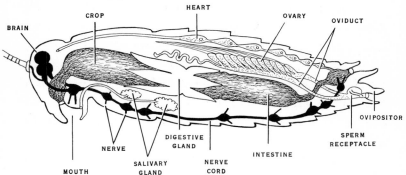

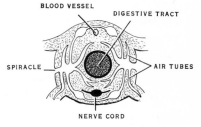

What a typical insect looks like inside. The crop stores food temporarily. The salivary gland helps to digest food, as does the larger gland around the intestine. Food wastes leave the body from the anus. The heart is simply a swelling in a large single blood vessel; actually, there are often several such swellings. The nerve cord and nerves control the bug's motions and organs. (For simplicity, nerves coming from the nerve cord are only indicated.) Though an insect has a brain, this is too small and undeveloped to do anything we would call thinking.

The ovary manufactures eggs, and these travel down the oviduct. They meet sperms that have been inserted in the sperm receptacle by a male insect, and these sperms start the development of the egg. Then the ovipositor drops the eggs, or, in the case of some insects, pushes them into earth or tree bark.

The cross-section picture shows an insect as if it were cut across the middle. The spiracles, or openings for breathing, are in the outer wall of the body, and tubes carry air all through the body.

It would be interesting at a club meeting to have one of the older members open a cocoon. The plump, brown, active pupa is an unusual object to see. Using a single-edge razor blade, carefully cut the cocoon in half and roll the pupa out in your hand. You can see the form of the antennae and thus tell whether it is a male or female. (The male antennae are wide and fernlike; the female ones are narrow.) Leave the pupa in the cocoon shell and it will open in due time.

While hunting for cocoons, you may find some interesting egg cases. The praying mantis egg case is one to take home and fasten to a bush in your yard. You will find galls or "oak apples" in many shapes and sizes. The larvas of a small gall wasp, feeding on the stems of the oak, stimulate the oak tissues to swell and produce these small round balls. Each ball may contain from one to six wasp larvas. During the summer, each larva changes to a pupa and then to an adult wasp. The wasp cuts a tiny hole in the gall with its mandibles and comes out to mate, lay eggs and begin another generation.

Examine the galls as you collect them. If you find holes, your specimen has already emerged. Hunt for different types of galls. Some look like warts or bumps on a stem. Keep each kind in a separate container labeled with the plant name, such as oak gall, goldenrod gall, rose gall, or blackberry gall. If you keep them in jars, you must have a fine net top. Some of the wasps are so small they may escape before you have a chance to compare them. Galls and their parasites make unusually interesting displays.

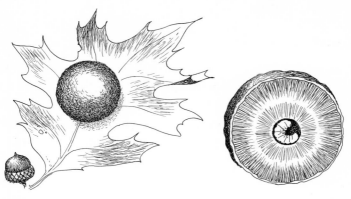

An oak gall, and the gall cut open to show the larva inside

Many adult insects die with the first frost, but a few hibernate, or sleep away the winter. Various kinds of beetles may be found under rocks or loose bark, or in thick piles of leaves. Hold one in your closely cupped hands and see how soon you feel a slight movement. Take another beetle into a warm room and see how quickly it revives (some insects may take a day or more). The club members might discuss other ways of experimenting with hibernating beetles and temperature changes. For instance, how long does it take an insect to "come to" in a room where the thermometer says 70 degrees, compared with the time it takes another of the same kind in a cellar at, let's say, 50 degrees? Or in a jar in the refrigerator at about 40 degrees? If you can find a rolled-up sowbug (not an insect, but related to them) among garden trash, put it near a radiator and presently it will pop open into its normal form.

The mourning cloak is the largest butterfly that hibernates as an adult. Look for it in boxes and barrels or other protected spots outdoors. Handle it carefully, as it appears stiff and lifeless. Take it into the house and see how soon it suddenly lifts its wings and flies around the room. See if you can find mosquitoes in the dark corners of a barn or cellar. Ants usually gather into a tight ball in their nests underground, though some can be found by themselves under loose bark. The queen bumblebee sleeps in her snug cave in the earth, or in a crevice in the rocks. Water striders crawl under trash around the edges of ponds and streams when the fall chill arrives.

In the eastern part of the United States, one kind of ladybug, the convergent lady beetle, sleeps in small cracks in foundations, chimneys, or rocks, or on an ivy-covered wall. In California they fly to mountaintops when winter comes and settle on bushes by the thousands. (Here they are gathered and shipped to farmers to help get rid of aphids and scale insects.)

The cabbage worm, larva of the cabbage butterfly, winters in a cocoon attached to a board or stone. The woolly bear caterpillar curls up in a tight ball under leaves or other plant trash. If you look carefully in a protected spot where the earth is soft you may be able to find tiny holes in which a grasshopper has laid eggs; you could try digging up a block of such earth if it isn't frozen and hatching grasshoppers indoors. In hunting for any of these insects, you may discover something new and exciting, for there is still much to be learned.

At your club meetings during the winter, learn some of the special words concerned with insects. Start with the

With games and special projects, winter need not stop a bug club.

word "entomology" and see how many know what it means. Someone will know that it is the study of insects. and that an "entomologist" is one who studies insects. Learn and use the Latin names for two or three butterflies: *Vanessa atalanta* is a grand name for the red admiral, and *Papilio glaucus* gives dignity to the tiger swallowtail.

Each week learn a new Latin name for some order (a certain grouping) of insect and talk about those you hope to find in this order. Eight of the orders contain many of the well-known insects:

Coleoptera	click beetles, prionus beetles, June bugs, ladybugs, Japanese beetles, tiger beetles
Diptera	mosquitoes, crane flies, robber flies, horseflies, fruit flies
Hemiptera	giant water bugs, shield bugs, milkweed bugs, harlequin bugs, waterboatmen
Hymenoptera	ants, wasps, hornets, bees
Lepidoptera	butterflies, moths, skippers
Neuroptera	lacewings, ant lions, dobsonflies
Odonata	dragonflies, damselflies
Orthoptera	katydids, crickets, cockroaches, grasshoppers, praying mantises

Latin is the language of the world for scientists. All animals and plants have Latin names as well as common names. The Latin name for the painted lady is *Vanessa cardui*. A French entomologist or a German entomologist or a Spanish entomologist may not know a butterfly by the name of "painted lady" but all three will know *Vanessa cardui*.

We invent many games at our meetings and you can do the same. One we always like we call "Name the Insect." Insects can be divided into four big groups:

1. Aerial—in the air.
2. Aquatic—in water.
3. Arboreal—in trees and bushes.
4. Terrestrial—on or in the ground.

The leader starts the game by pointing at a member and saying, "aerial." The member must quickly name an insect that is found in the air, such as dragonfly, monarch, or firefly. If he answers correctly, he is *it* and points his finger and perhaps says, "terrestrial." The answer can be stinkbug, grasshopper, or ants. Some insects fit equally well in two classes and this leads to much discussion.

"Building a Nature Museum" is fun and extremely difficult in spots. Each member names an insect for each letter of the alphabet, beginning with *a*. The leader starts by saying, "We're going to build a nature museum, and I'll bring an ant. What will you bring?" The next one can say bug or butterfly. Then come caterpillar, doodlebug, earwig, and so on. Several letters will be a little difficult but probably *x* is the only one you will have to omit.

"Building a House" creates a lot of discussion and new ideas. Each member may make a suggestion and, if no one has a reply, must defend his suggestion with an answer. Here are some of the suggestions and answers that we use:

We'll need an aviator to make an aerial survey.
    Dragonfly is a good answer.

We'll need to consult architects.	*Bees.*
Someone must do the excavating.	*Mole cricket.*
We can use many carpenters.	*Ants.*
We'll need some electricians.	*Fireflies.*

We'll want some drillers.	*Ichneumon flies.*
We might need a tent to cover our supplies.	*Tent caterpillars.*
We must watch for robbers and thieves.	*Robber flies and dung beetles.*
We'll hire a guard.	*Bombardier beetle.*
We'll need some paper.	*Wasps.*
We'll need cement.	*Mud daubers.*
We may need a tunnel under the house.	*Termites.*
We'll need a few gardeners for the yard.	*Leaf-cutting ants.*

An old favorite in a new form is "Who Am I?" It can be played two ways. The person who is *it* leaves the room and the members decide he is a dragonfly. They call him back and he asks one after another, "Who am I?" The object is to give as many clues as possible without giving away the answer. After each clue, *it* tries to guess who he is. The clues can be: you have four wings; you have large eyes; sometimes you're green; sometimes you have blue spots; you live near water, etc. Clues that would give away the answer quickly are: you live in water for a year or two; you fly like a small jet. A second way to play this game is to let the one who is *it* decide who he is. One by one the members ask him, "Who are you?" and he gives the clues. The one who guesses the answer becomes *it*. These games encourage reading and looking for detail in pictures for extra material for clues.

"Friends and Foes" is a game that has no end as you learn more and more about insects. If there is a blackboard available, write the two words "friends" and "foes" to head the lists of two kinds of insects. The members make suggestions and tell how the insect is a friend of human beings or why it is a foe.

FRIENDS	FOES
ladybug	*cockroach*
bumblebee	*mosquito*
praying mantis	*tent caterpillar*
butterfly	*weevil*
ichneumon fly	*grasshopper*
lacewing	*Japanese beetle*
dragonfly	*termite*

Anyone can challenge whether an insect named is a friend or a foe. If he challenges, he must have a reason and explain it. Some insects are both friend and foe but a little more of one than the other. The grasshopper as a foe can be challenged, for there are some tribes in Africa that depend on grasshoppers as their main food supply. On the other hand, grasshoppers often destroy huge crops and bring famine to people.

A challenging game, "Questions," is one in which each member is asked to bring a question to the next meeting. This leads to long discussions, as some questions have more than one answer.

What insect keeps a "cow"?	*Ant.*
What insect works like an electric fan?	*Bee.*
What does a silk moth eat?	*It doesn't eat.*
Name three insects we like.	*Ladybugs, honeybees, praying mantises.*
Name three harmful insects.	*Japanese beetles, weevils, cabbage butterflies.*
What insect is born and dies the same day?	*Mayfly.*
What insect song grows louder as the day gets hotter?	*Cicada.*
What is a naiad?	*The young of a dragonfly, damselfly, mayfly, or stonefly.*
What is a nymph?	*The young of an insect that doesn't become a larva and pupa as it grows up.*
What insect sings at night?	*Cricket.*

One morning you will look out the window to find the sun shining, the snow melting, the birds singing, and

Ants keep aphids as "cows"; they extract from them a liquid called honeydew.

one lone mourning cloak fluttering across the yard. The winter games have served their purpose, and it's time to shake out the net and go hunting for bugs again.

Bug Exhibits and Prizes

The end of summer is the time for a bug-club exhibit. We announce months ahead of time that we will have our big exhibit on the last Saturday in September. During the summer we talk about the kinds of exhibits to be planned and how they will be judged. We feel that each member should have an award for participating. Mothers and big sisters can cut blue, red, and white ribbons and mark them with India ink as first, second, and third prizes, and honorable mention. Or plain cards can be hand printed or typed. If there are enough entries, each classification can receive all four awards. We give awards for the following classifications:

> BEST IN SHOW
> MOST ORIGINAL
> GENERAL COLLECTION
> SPECIAL COLLECTION

BEST IN PRESENTATION
LIVE INSECTS
BEST HOMEMADE EQUIPMENT
LIFE CYCLE
MOST UNUSUAL FOREIGN COLLECTION
BEGINNERS

BEST IN SHOW is something the judge will decide. It can be an exhibit from any one of the classes or something entirely different. It may show thoughtful planning, extra work, or creative individuality. One year this award was given to the boy who exchanged 650 polyphemus cocoons for a striking collection of foreign beetles, grasshoppers, walkingsticks, and jungle mantises. They were well displayed in glass-covered cases and were a complete exhibit by themselves. BEST IN SHOW can be as simple as half a dozen butterflies of the same species, carefully mounted and labeled, showing differences in size and color patterns. Fritillary butterflies (which have very spotted wings and stand on only four legs) have unusual changes in color. One member raised nearly a hundred, and collected six with odd color patterns.

MOST ORIGINAL is usually a complete surprise. I'll never forget the first one at our club. It was a small cardboard box in which a nine-year-old sprinkled some sand, added a few small rocks, twigs, and flowers for a garden scene, and in one corner a single monarch butterfly mounted in a natural flying position. This was as simple and beautiful as a poem.

When exhibition time comes, you'll be glad you took the trouble to make your exhibit carefully.

A GENERAL COLLECTION includes carefully mounted and labeled butterflies, moths, beetles, true bugs, wasps, ants, dragonflies—everything commonly found in the area. The adult visitors will be amazed that so many such creatures live in and around their yards.

A SPECIAL COLLECTION is a class that interests both beginners and older members. This can be as modest as four or five dragonflies. If not crowded in a killing jar, dragonflies usually die with their wings in perfect position. Catching four or five dragonflies sounds simple but wait until you try it. They zip past like small jets, and you

The eyed elater, or click beetle, is a fine acrobat.

need a quick eye and a fast swoop to capture one. Instead of using cigar boxes, try pinning dragonflies on cattails or other plants gathered at the pond or stream where you caught them.

Another special collection is one of caterpillar skin molts, or of empty cocoons and chrysalises, or a collection of butterfly and moth eggs. Eggs are kept by pouring hot paraffin over them. Label them with species name, plant food, and date found. Chrysalises are as varied in size and shape as sea shells. Many empty ones remain whole but lose most of their color. Cocoons come in interesting sizes and shapes, too. Label them like the chrysalises and, if possible, the date they opened.

When a caterpillar molts, the old skin shrinks to almost nothing but retains its individuality. The six tiny feet with claws usually show plainly. And with the skin, keep the tiny face mask that drops off separately. Labeled and in Riker mounts, they make an exceptional display.

A praying mantis molts six or seven times. These paper-thin tan skeletons, each larger than the last, retain their size and shape, looking like straggly ghosts.

BEST IN PRESENTATION is the most professional exhibit. Each insect should be a perfect specimen and each at the same height on the pin; labels should be clearly printed and all in line. There are always a few in a club who enjoy close, meticulous work. These members often specialize in science when they get to college.

LIVE INSECTS are always impressive, and an easy class for beginners. With special cages or containers, these create a great deal of interest. One of the best displays is one species of caterpillar at different stages of growth; a few small ones, one fully grown, one hanging up for the final molt, and the completed chrysalis. If a few eggs are added, plus a mounted adult, you have an A-1 exhibit. This is the kind a seven- or eight-year-old can be proud to display. Butterfly eggs are not hard to get. When you are collecting in the field, stand still and watch a butterfly near you. If she lights on a plant for a few moments, then wings away to others, you can guess that she is laying eggs. They may be on top of the leaf or underneath.

A live insect that can steal the show is that amazing performer, the click beetle. It is easy to give a demonstration for an audience. Lay the beetle upside down on a table. It thrashes its legs wildly for a few seconds. Then it arches its back and with a loud *click!* it flips into the air and comes down on its feet. Sometimes it will land on its back and may have to click and bounce several times before it lands on its feet. There are click beetles everywhere but, if possible, try to find the elegant "eyed" elater for display. It is a striking gray-black beetle with two large black spots on its thorax that suggest eyes. You can keep one in your terrarium. It will need a bit of decayed wood to chew and will also nibble on banana or any soft fruit.

BEST HOMEMADE EQUIPMENT will show others they do not need to buy from stores. Have each piece labeled and explain to the visitors how it is used. There should be a butterfly net, a killing jar, a spreading board, and a cigar box with a few pinned insects. Have a fresh butterfly on the spreading board. One side of the butterfly can be pinned and the other side used to demonstrate how the mounting and pinning are done. This performance will draw many interested adults as well as children.

LIFE CYCLE is a fascinating display. This can be made up of live or dead specimens. One year, one of the older members showed polyphemus eggs; fat, lime-green caterpillars eating birch leaves; one caterpillar spinning its cocoon; and a live moth in its rich brown color with pink and blue trim.

Dead caterpillars can be shown in a pill bottle of alcohol, or they can be dropped in a killing jar the day before the exhibit and used in a display. Of course the caterpillars from the killing jar cannot be kept, as they will soon deteriorate. Caterpillars can be preserved by the method of inflation. This is difficult to do without the necessary apparatus but is interesting to try once. Here is a simple method that works fairly well if you are patient.

Use a full-grown caterpillar; a smooth one like a swallowtail caterpillar is easier to handle than a hairy one. Put the caterpillar in your killing jar for about half an hour. Remove it and place on a large blotter. Using a round smooth object such as a round pencil, start at the head and roll the pencil gently the full length of the body to remove the contents of the abdomen. Continue to roll and press gently until all is removed. The next step is to inflate and dry the empty skin. You will need a common eyedropper with the rubber end removed. Insert this into the opening through which the contents were removed and blow gently until the skin is rounded out into normal size. Without losing any air, slip your thumb over the end that is in your mouth. Hold the skin over a low gas flame and turn it from side to side as it dries. This is a tedious job and if you tire before the skin is thoroughly dry, you have to inflate it and try again. Once the skin is dry it will retain its roundness. The eyedropper may stick to the skin and should be carefully loosened with a needle or pin. The skin will lose much of its color and can be touched up with dime-store water colors. This caterpillar

in a Riker mount with an egg, a chrysalis, and a mounted butterfly will give you a real feeling of accomplishment.

MOST UNUSUAL FOREIGN COLLECTION consists of insects purchased from a hobby shop or supply house. These insects are dry and break easily. Butterflies and moths have folded wings and come in small envelopes. They must be completely relaxed and mounted. It is advisable to display a relaxing jar with one dry butterfly. In this way the visitors will understand how much work goes into the collection.

BEGINNERS should be encouraged and helped in every way. If they are going to enter something in the exhibit, they must do their own work so they can enjoy a feeling of accomplishment. Six- and seven-year-olds often have an intense interest and want desperately to try what the older ones are doing. Let them try and they'll learn fast.

A local science teacher can be invited to judge the show, or a high school student who has collected insects, or a 4-H or Boy Scout leader who has a personal interest in insects. The members should invite their friends to come, their parents and their teachers. The local paper will often send a photographer to cover the event. A bug-club exhibit can be real news.

Each member should show only his best. No torn wings, no missing antennae, all six legs showing on bugs and beetles. When live insects are displayed, they must be in proper cages or containers and have fresh food. Each member should be prepared to answer questions and give explanations about collecting and mounting insects.

The first meeting after the big exhibit will be full of talk. At this time it is interesting to ask each member what he would like to accomplish in the coming year. Keep a record of these statements in your attendance book and check them a year later. Here are a few resolutions from the Hayward Library Bug Club:

Find and raise a walkingstick.

Label all my insects.

Build a large collection of beetles.

Catch a giant water bug with eggs on his back.

Raise silkworms and unwind a silk thread from the cocoon.

Collect and classify at least eighty insects.

Watch an adult dragonfly come out of its nymph skin.

A Note to Parents and Teachers

A ten-year-old boy walked up to my desk in the Hayward Public Library, held out a small brown object about the size of his little finger, and asked, "What is this?"

It was dry and hard to my touch and looked like an odd piece of weathered wood. I thought I knew what it was and replied, "It looks like a butterfly chrysalis."

"Of course," said the boy, "but what *kind* of butterfly?"

I didn't know but it was something I had always wanted to know. The boy left the chrysalis on my desk and the more I looked at it, the more intrigued I became about the unknown answer. Several boys had been asking for a science club to meet in the library once a week. We had a weekly story hour, why not a science club?

And this being the sort of activity that any teacher or parent may well want to help along, as active leader or behind-the-scenes adviser, perhaps I should say a few words to nature-minded adults. My experiences with the library club should be a practical help.

When a high school senior volunteered to plan the meetings and make spreading boards, I thought it was a fine idea. I called the local newspaper and asked if they would print a notice inviting "all boys and girls interested in insects to attend the first meeting in the library club room next Friday at four o'clock."

That was many years ago, and the Bug Club has been meeting every Friday at four o'clock since, except for the three or four weeks that I go on vacation each year. Five girls and fifteen boys, ages seven to twelve, came to that first meeting. We decided the club would concentrate on insects, as one hour a week wouldn't be enough time to study snakes, lizards, frogs, and all the other interesting creatures that children discover and carry home. For three months I watched with amazement as those children sat and listened to a high-school boy lecture on the balance of nature, incomplete metamorphosis, etc.

Suddenly school was out, his draft number came up, and the club was all mine. I was as new and inexperienced as the children concerning such things as killing jars, relaxing methods, and mounting techniques. There was no need to worry about planned meetings. The children brought so many specimens and asked so many questions that we worked and learned together. Fortunately the California Academy of Sciences is less than an hour away. The entomology department was more than helpful.

One of the first things we needed was a few good books for identification. The two we found most helpful are big, solid adult books: Essig's *Insects of Western North America* and Comstock's *Introduction to Entomology*. An intent little second-grader can use the illustrations in these books to good advantage. I learned this from a serious little seven-year-old. He asked for a book on atoms. I took him to the science shelf and said, "I don't think any of these books are written on your grade level. I'm afraid you can't read them." He reached for a book and said, in a tone of voice I will never forget, "Who cares about reading? I want to look at the pictures."

One small boy in the Bug Club could find pictures for us for nearly every strange insect that was brought in. For the first year or two, nearly all of them were strange and odd-looking bugs. Now, after ten years, we are delighted when an unknown caterpillar or beetle is found. And they are still found. Even twenty to thirty youngsters collecting insects every week for years cannot uncover all the possibilities that an area has to offer. This element of surprise is like a game of chance; one never knows what will turn up next. And for the youngsters, it is always the hope that they will find something rare and unusual. Over and over again I hear the excited "Look what I found. Do you think this is rare?"

In the club we encourage everyone to raise as many of his specimens as possible. Members learn how and where to hunt for the eggs and raise the caterpillars, waiting for that magic moment when the creeping crea-

These bugs are somewhat rare, but you may find them. At top, a stag beetle; at bottom, a walkingstick.

ture is suddenly transformed into an immobile chrysalis. Raising large silk moths is a somewhat different experience. When a youngster finds a large moth and she lays eggs, the chances are the eggs are fertile, as the moths usually mate within the first twenty-four hours. When a grown caterpillar starts to spin a cocoon, one can watch the work for two or three days before the cocoon is solid. One day it is soft and silvery, the next day brown and firm. The caterpillar wets it with a fluid that hardens it for winter protection. Watching a silk moth emerge from its cocoon is a dramatic and startling sight.

Younger members are encouraged to collect the less fragile insects, such as beetles and grasshoppers and ants. After learning to handle them easily, they go on to the

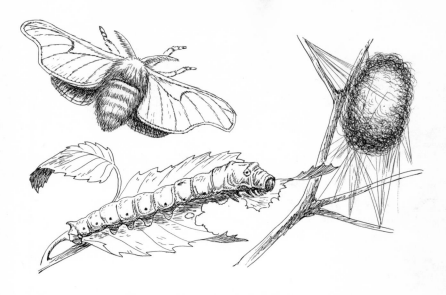

A silkworm, silk moth, and cocoon

more exacting task of mounting butterflies and moths. Anyone is welcome to come to the club meetings, but to be a true club member one has to contribute two perfect specimens for the library collection. This collection is a permanent display in a glass case in the corner of the room. When a parent is hunting for a missing child, he is often found sitting in front of this case.

In California we have about eight months of the year for insect collecting. These months are spent in identifying live insects, studying their life cycles, learning how to collect and keep them. During the other months we read about insects in books and magazines. We learn a few special words like "Lepidoptera," *"Papilio,"* "terrestrial," and "entomologist." Children love to use big words casually. We talk about the insects that are our friends and those that are our foes and the role that each plays in our lives. We play many guessing games about insects, some of them made up on the spur of the moment. These are described in the chapter on fall and winter activities. During the winter months we also collect cocoons and send to supply houses for species that are not native to our area. Local hobby shops or toy stores may carry spreading boards, nets, and insect pins. If they do not have them, the news that a club is starting may persuade the owner to stock these items.

During most of the year, there is a live project in evidence in the junior room in our library. This live exhibit not only brings the children back to the library every week, but a great many adults come back to check on the progress. We have successfully raised ant lions, dragonflies, praying mantises, and practically every caterpillar found in the area. A small square fish bowl makes a satisfactory terrarium for these projects.

A praying mantis, raised from the egg case in April to an extreme old age in February, drew the biggest following. As many adults as children made special trips to the library with a fly or a grasshopper or other juicy morsel to feed the mantis.

It is almost impossible to limit a club to insects only. While collecting insects, many other interesting creatures are discovered and cannot be completely bypassed. The most spectacular of these was a large hairy tarantula from the desert. When a boy asked if we would

keep it in the library for a week, I hesitated until I contacted the California Academy of Sciences. On being told that this species was practically harmless, we put the tarantula in a terrarium with a tight screen covering, placed it on the desk and waited for repercussions. During the two weeks it remained in the room, we met more fathers than we usually see in six months. They found it difficult to believe their children and came in to see for themselves. They looked skeptical and stayed to read about tarantulas in encyclopedias and other books.

Parents and teachers will find the fostering of a bug club (or any nature club) a rewarding experience. The only requirement is that the leader have as much enthusiasm for the subject as the members. Learning with the children is more fun than knowing all the answers in advance. Teachers may discover that children will gladly stay after school once a week to study and share their insect discoveries with others. Parents may start by inviting a few neighborhood children to a back-yard meeting. The news will spread rapidly from door to door, block to block. Nearly all children at some time in their lives have a natural curiosity about the crawling, squirming animal life in their yards that is either ignored or considered a nuisance.

An adult should not hesitate to form a club because of his lack of knowledge of the subject. Knowledge will grow with doing and sharing. Learning with the youngsters will be a stimulating challenge. There are excellent books for beginners that will answer most initial questions. There will be some questions, of course, that have elusive answers. If there is a nature museum, university, or college in your area, a visit to the entomology department will be helpful. A friendly welcome and a quick answer to most questions will be the result.

Publicity of course helps a club to grow. Local newspapers are usually pleased to get human-interest stories. To help start a club, phone and ask for the city editor, or get in touch with a local reporter if you know one. Tell what you are planning to do and why, give the place, day, and hour of meetings, and say who is invited. If you have a small group already started with some collecting equipment and a few insects, the paper may want to come and take a picture. Many stores will welcome a small window display of mounted insects and an attractive poster inviting children to join the club.

You may sometimes find that a few members (or even you yourself) have a lingering feeling that insects are "creepy" and unpleasant. There's nothing like familiarity to help them over this notion, and it will dissolve away as they handle and observe. Watching a caterpillar through a complete life cycle can give both young people and adults a new feeling of respect and awe for the "creepy, crawly creatures."

There are probably more insects than any other kind of many-celled animals on the face of the earth (though some scientists hold out for the tiny marine crustaceans called copepods). Collecting them is a fine hobby for

A mantis is often a very popular exhibit.

children, partly because it's almost impossible to over-collect in any area. While they are collecting insects, children will learn something about trees, birds, snakes, frogs, lizards, spiders, and many other things in nature.

I would like to enter a strong plea for parents to try to understand and sympathize with their children's nature interests. They are often a changing attraction that may go through many phases. Boys may go from caterpillars to frogs to snakes to hawks. Each stage may be solidly serious to the youngster at the time. As part of it he should be encouraged to care for his captives. If parents would patiently teach their children to care for their pets correctly, everyone concerned could be happy about them. The time to start is when little Johnny or Mary puts the first caterpillar into a jar. They should be taught that a caterpillar needs fresh leaves and a clean jar every day. If they don't care for their caterpillars, they should turn them loose.

Collecting insects is a world-wide hobby engaged in by more adults than children. Many adults have a dormant interest in nature. It's never too late for an adult to start a bug club. And whether it's one for grown-ups or youngsters, some happy adult is going to find himself recapturing some of the wonders of childhood.

More Books to Read

Insect Life (Boy Scout Merit Badge pamphlet).

Junior Book of Insects, by Edwin Way Teale (Dutton, 1953).

Butterflies and Moths, by Robert T. Mitchell and Herbert S. Zim (Golden Press, 1964).

The Insect Guide, by Ralph W. Swain (Doubleday, 1948).

Insects, by Herbert S. Zim and Clarence Cottam (Golden Press, 1956).

Collecting Cocoons, by Lois J. Hussing and Catherine Pessino (Crowell, 1953).

Supply Houses

BUTTERFLY ART JEWELRY, INC.
291 East 98 St.
Brooklyn 12, New York City
(*All kinds of insect equipment sold,
not just jewelry.*)

THE LEMBERGER CO.
P. O. Box 482
Oshkosh, Wisconsin

WARD'S OF CALIFORNIA
Box 1749
Monterey, California

WARD'S NATURAL SCIENCE ESTABLISHMENT
P. O. Box 1712
Rochester, New York 14603

Index

Index